AIR COMMAND AND ST/
AIR UNIVERS

The Expeditionary Airfield as a Center of Gravity

Henderson Field during the Guadalcanal Campaign (August 1942–February 1943)

JEFF D. PHILIPPART
Major, USAF

Air Command and Staff College
Wright Flyer Paper No. 19

Air University Press
Maxwell Air Force Base, Alabama

September 2004

> This Wright Flyer Paper and others in the series are available electronically at the Air University Research Web site http://research.maxwell.af.mil and the AU Press Web site http://aupress.maxwell.af.mil.

Disclaimer

Opinions, conclusions, and recommendations expressed or implied within are solely those of the author and do not necessarily represent the views of Air University, the United States Air Force, the Department of Defense, or any other US government agency. Cleared for public release: distribution unlimited.

Foreword

It is my great pleasure to present another of the *Wright Flyer Papers* series. In this series, Air Command and Staff College (ACSC) recognizes and publishes our best student research projects from the prior academic year. The ACSC research program encourages our students to move beyond the school's core curriculum in their own professional development and in "advancing air and space power." The series title reflects our desire to perpetuate the pioneering spirit embodied in earlier generations of Airmen. Projects selected for publication combine solid research, innovative thought, and lucid presentation in exploring war at the operational level. With this broad perspective, the *Wright Flyer Papers* engage an eclectic range of doctrinal, technological, organizational, and operational questions. Some of these studies provide new solutions to familiar problems. Others encourage us to leave the familiar behind in pursuing new possibilities. By making these research studies available in the *Wright Flyer Papers*, ACSC hopes to encourage critical examination of the findings and to stimulate further research in these areas.

RONALD R. LADNIER
Brigadier General, USAF
Commandant

Preface

My initial interest in the topic of Guadalcanal came from my grandfather, Lt Col J. E. Estes, USMC, retired, who fought on the 'Canal with the 2d Marine Division. I also wanted to relate a historical example from World War II to some of my recent experiences in expeditionary combat operations throughout Operations Enduring Freedom and Iraqi Freedom. During the course of my research, I was amazed at the truly joint nature of the Guadalcanal campaign. Each branch of service contributed to the eventual victory over the Japanese. This campaign was especially compelling because each side won tactical victories, and the ultimate victor was in doubt for months. Even senior American leaders, such as Gen Douglas MacArthur and Adm Robert Lee Ghormley, doubted the Marines could maintain their foothold in the Solomons. After six months of battle, the Americans defeated the Japanese. This victory was the turning point of the war in the Pacific. After Guadalcanal, the Japanese fought on the strategic defensive for the remainder of the war.

I am indebted to my advisor, Dr. Richard Muller, for his thoughtful advice and absolute passion for the history of World War II. I greatly appreciate the staff of the Air University Library and Air Force Historical Research Agency for their assistance in my quest for research material. I thank my wife, Erin, and our sons, Jackson and Benjamin, for their constant support and tremendous patience. I thank the men and women of the "greatest generation," especially my grandparents, who fought for freedom and sacrificed so much during World War II.

Abstract

This study explores the contemporary relevance of the Guadalcanal campaign to current military operations. Specifically, it uses expeditionary joint air operations flown from Henderson Field during the period August 1942 to February 1943 as a case study for the employment of airpower from an austere airfield. Henderson Field provides a historical example of the expeditionary airfield as a center of gravity for joint military operations, and it demonstrates that key force enablers provide critical capabilities for the use of airpower from austere airfields. The joint air forces at Henderson Field, collectively known as the Cactus Air Force, flew defensive counterair and interdiction missions against the Japanese. The Cactus Air Force also provided close air support for US Marines fighting against the Japanese army on Guadalcanal. Air operations from this austere airfield would not have been possible without several key force enablers. Maintenance, logistics, and runway construction and repair were vital to sustaining the outnumbered Cactus Air Force. US Marine and Army ground troops—who fought multiple battles to protect Henderson Field—provided airfield security. In the dramatic course of this seesaw campaign, the tactical capabilities of the Cactus Air Force were key to the eventual victory by the Americans.

The contributions of the Cactus Air Force and the American victory during the Guadalcanal campaign changed the course of World War II in the Pacific. After Guadalcanal the Japanese military never regained the strategic offensive. The lessons from Henderson Field also have direct relevance to current expeditionary air operations. Recent military operations in Afghanistan and Iraq could not have succeeded without the combat airpower employed from expeditionary air bases. The US Air Force recognizes the value of combat support as evidenced by the recent introduction of Eagle Flag exercises, which practice the art of establishing austere bases. Thus, the importance of the employment of joint airpower from austere bases around the world is magnified by the global war against terrorism. Henderson Field provides an example of successful expeditionary joint air operations that is relevant to the planners of future military operations.

Introduction

A petition with more than 8,000 signatures—including many veterans from World War II—was delivered during the summer of 2003 to the prime minister of the Solomon Islands. This petition requested the government reverse a decision to rename the international airport the chrysanthemum, which is the Japanese national flower.[1] The airfield, originally named Henderson Field, was a centerpiece to one of the epic campaigns fought during World War II. These veterans, after more than 60 years, easily recalled the importance of Henderson Field in the fight to prevent Japanese expansion and in the establishment of a foothold for US forces in the South Pacific. This recent controversy in the Solomons raises several questions, especially in light of the increased importance of expeditionary joint military operations to conduct a global war against terrorism.

- What was the significance of Henderson Field to the Guadalcanal campaign?
- What capabilities did the air forces that operated from this austere airfield bring to the fight for Guadalcanal?
- What were the key enablers that allowed airpower to function in such a challenging environment?
- What relevance do Henderson Field and the Guadalcanal campaign have for current expeditionary military operations?

Henderson Field was a center of gravity (COG) during the Guadalcanal campaign. Joint doctrine defines COGs as, "those characteristics, capabilities, or sources of power from which a military force derives its freedom of action, physical strength, or will to fight."[2] Airplanes that operated from Henderson Field provided the joint military forces with significant tactical capabilities, which included defensive counterair (DCA), interdiction, and close air support (CAS). The Japanese military recognized that Henderson Field was a COG during the course of the campaign as they repeatedly attacked the air base with ground assaults and air and naval bombardment. Importantly, with the current focus of the US Air Force on conducting expeditionary military operations, Henderson Field provides several lessons that are relevant to contemporary military planners. Key force enablers (e.g.,

2 EXPEDITIONARY AIRFIELD AS CENTER OF GRAVITY

maintenance, runway repair, and airfield security) were vital to air operations from Henderson Field during the Guadalcanal campaign. These force enablers remain vital in the use of airpower from contemporary expeditionary air bases. Thus, Henderson Field provides a historical example of the expeditionary airfield as a COG for joint military operations. It also demonstrates that key force enablers provide the critical capabilities for the use of airpower from austere airfields.

Henderson Field, Guadalcanal. Photographed from a USS *Saratoga* (CV-3) plane in the latter part of August 1942, after US aircraft had begun to use the airfield. The view looks about northwest, with the Lunga River running across the upper portion of the image. Iron Bottom Sound is just out of view at the top. Several planes are parked to the left, and numerous bomb and shell craters are visible.

Background

The United States entered World War II after Japan's devastating surprise attack on Pearl Harbor in December 1941. The Japanese seized the initiative following the attack on Pearl Harbor and rapidly expanded their empire in the Pacific. Within months Japan had successfully taken the Philippines from the United States and Singapore from Great Britain in addition to many other islands and territories throughout the Pacific region. This so-called Greater East Asia Co-Prosperity Sphere extended to Rabaul in New Britain and the Solomon Islands. From this position in the South Pacific, the Japanese were in a prime position to capture Port Moresby and threaten Australia. Eventually, the US military adopted a two-prong strategy of attack in the Pacific with Adm Chester W. Nimitz's navy striking from the waters of the central Pacific and Gen Douglas MacArthur leading US troops in the islands of the southwest Pacific. Because of widespread public desire for revenge, US military and political leaders feared the threat of Nazi Germany more than that of Japan, and the United States officially adopted a Germany-first strategy for World War II at the beginning of 1942.

In contrast to the Army's focus on Germany first, Adm Ernest J. King, the chief of naval operations, concentrated on the Pacific and the war against Japan. King and his planning staff spent the first half of 1942 revising war plans for the Pacific theater. They also focused on protecting Australia and the line of communications in the South Pacific. By 2 July 1942, in spite of bureaucratic wrangling between the US Army and US Navy, the Joint Chiefs of Staff (JCS) agreed to a plan (code-named Pestilence) to retake the Solomons and Rabaul. Phase one of this plan was called Operation Watchtower, and it required the US Navy to lead amphibious operations to seize Tulagi Island and the Santa Cruz Islands.[3] On 5 July American radio intelligence and aerial reconnaissance indicated the Japanese were building an airfield on the island of Guadalcanal.[4] Upon receiving this news, Admiral King and Admiral Nimitz, combatant commander, Pacific Fleet, scratched the Santa Cruz Islands from phase one and inserted Guadalcanal. D-day for Operation Watchtower was initially set for 1 August, but a delay in loading the transport ships forced D-day to slip almost a week. The carrier and amphibious task forces met off the coast of the Fiji Islands at the end of July for a rehearsal before sailing northwest for Tulagi and Guadalcanal. As the ships left Fiji, Vice Adm Robert Lee Ghormley, commander of the South Pacific Fleet, sent the following mes-

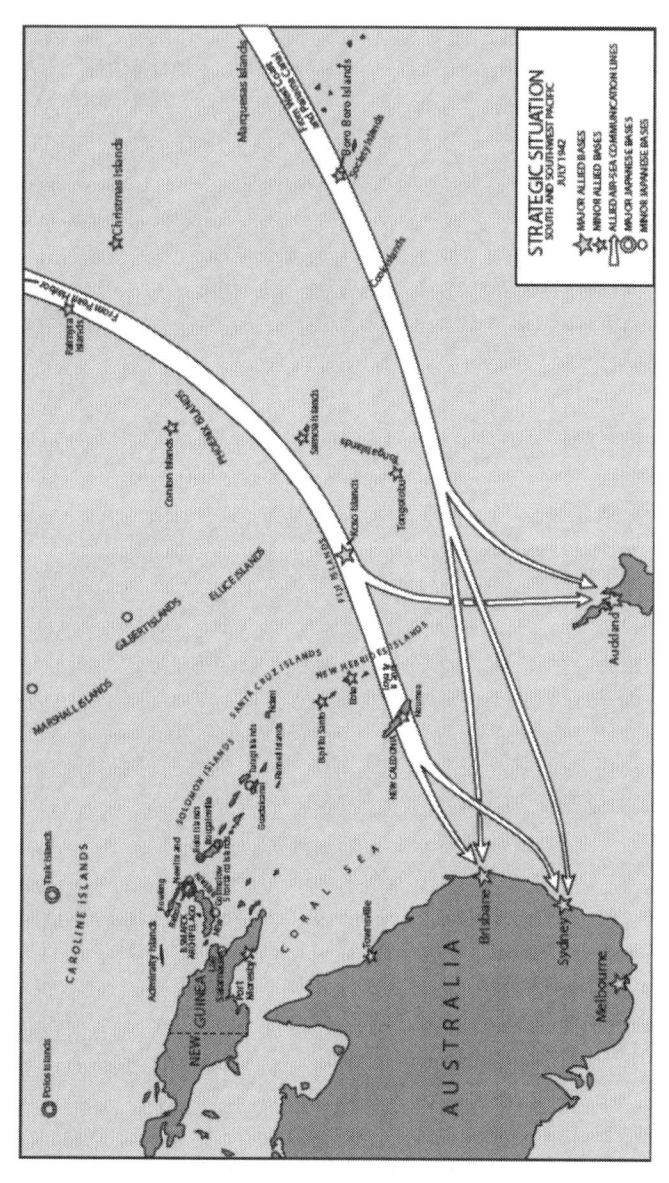

Sea Line of Communications (LOC) in South Pacific. The closeness of Guadalcanal to the major sea LOCs from Hawaii and California to Australia and New Zealand is shown. Thus, the construction of a Japanese airfield on Guadalcanal represented a serious strategic threat to the Allies in July 1942. (Reprinted from http://www.army.mil/cmh-pg/books/wwii/guadc/gc-fm.htm.)

sage: "We look to you to electrify the world. . . . Sock 'em in the Solomons."[5]

With Admiral King's persistent influence, the US military went on the offensive for the first time in World War II to deny Japan access to island bases in the southern Solomons. Task Force 62, led by Adm Richmond Kelly Turner, landed on the beaches of Guadalcanal on the revised D-day, 7 August 1942.[6] Japanese military leaders were surprised by the attack because they did not expect America to launch offensive operations until 1943.[7] With the advantage of strategic and tactical surprise, the Marines encountered little resistance as they crossed the beaches of Guadalcanal. The Marines occupied the unfinished airfield at Lunga Point by the end of the second day as most of the 2,200 Japanese construction workers fled into the jungles.[8] The Marines had arrived the exact moment the Japanese had finished the ends of the airfield, and they expected their first fighter aircraft to arrive by mid-August.[9] Thus, with minimal time for planning and preparation, the Marines succeeded in removing a serious threat to Australia and the vital shipping lanes between the United States and the South Pacific. However, the Japanese would make holding the island much more difficult than the initial amphibious assault. Neither side expected the seesaw battle that occurred during the remainder of 1942.

Japan reacted swiftly to the news of an attack on Guadalcanal and launched bomber and fighter attacks from their bases in Rabaul against the Americans on the afternoon of 7 August. While the Navy's carrier fighters blunted the first waves of Japan's counterattack, Adm Frank J. Fletcher's Carrier Task Force 61 provided air support for the amphibious landing. Based on a contentious decision made during the rehearsal for Operation Watchtower, Admiral Fletcher ordered his carriers to depart the area on the second day of the operation.[10] Without air cover to occupy the Japanese bombers, Admiral Turner decided to stop off-loading cargo from his transports even though they were only halfway finished. Turner's decision to leave Guadalcanal was further reinforced by the heavy US Navy losses during the Battle of Savo Island in the early hours of 9 August.[11] Thus, Maj Gen Archer A. Vandegrift and the almost 17,000 Marines under his command were

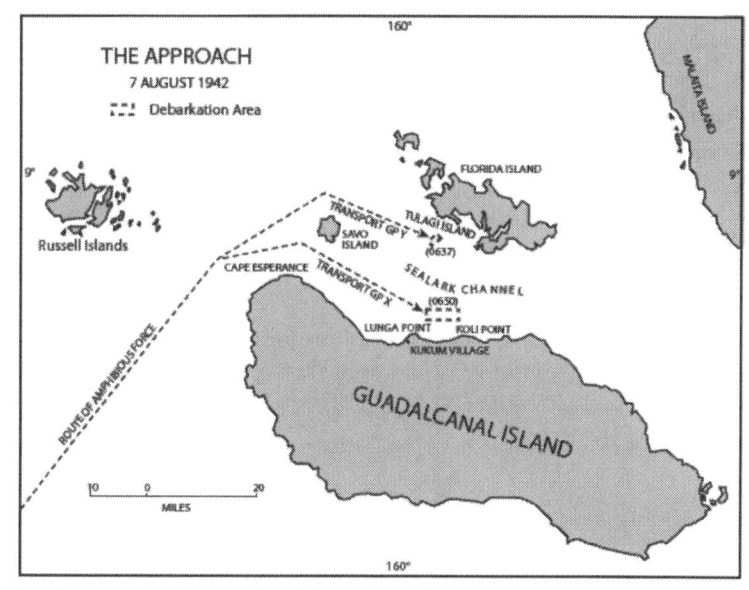

Amphibious Assault on Guadalcanal and Tulagi, 7 August 1942. This is the approach route of Task Force 62 for the amphibious landings on Tulagi and Guadalcanal. Tulagi was significant due to its deep-water harbor and Japanese seaplane base. (Reprinted from http://www.army.mil/cmh-pg/books/wwii/guadc/gc-fm.htm.)

left to defend the island with minimal supplies, no heavy artillery, and no air support.[12] For nearly two weeks and with no way to fight back effectively, the Marines suffered through unrelenting Japanese bomber and fighter attacks.

With the departure of air support and the unexpected lack of supplies, General Vandegrift knew completion of the airfield was the key to long-term survival.[13] By 18 August the Marines of the First Engineer Battalion completed the airfield (3,778 feet long and 150 feet wide) at Lunga Point. During its construction, the Marines chose the name Henderson Field to honor Maj Lofton Henderson, a Marine pilot and squadron commander who died in the Battle of Midway.[14] On 20 August planes from Marine Air Group (MAG) 23 launched from the escort carrier USS *Long Island* and arrived at Henderson Field. This initial group from MAG 23 included 12 Douglas shipborne dive-bombers (SBD) from Marine Bombing Squadron (VMSB) 232 and 19 Grumman F4F Wildcats from Marine Fighting Squadron

(VMF) 223. The Marines cheered loudly as these first planes arrived. General Vandegrift told Maj Richard Mangrum, the first pilot from the group to land, "Thank God you have come."[15] MAG 23 was soon joined by 14 P-400s (an export version of the P-39) from the Army Air Force's 67th Fighter Squadron. This assortment of planes was part of Marine Air Wing 1 (MAW-1), but they were unofficially labeled the Cactus Air Force, in reference to the American code name Cactus, for Guadalcanal.

Tactical Capabilities of Henderson Field—Defensive Counterair

Henderson Field and the airpower of the Cactus Air Force provided significant tactical advantages for the US forces fighting to maintain a foothold on Guadalcanal. During most of the campaign, the primary mission of the Cactus Air Force was to intercept Japanese bombers and fighters. The men of the Cactus force were fighting a defensive battle to protect their turf. They knew Henderson Field was a primary target for almost every Japanese bombing mission. The fighters would receive word of inbound enemy aircraft from their early warning radar or from forward observers called coast watchers. The Royal Australian Navy trained the coast watchers prior to World War II, and they were located throughout the Solomon Islands.[16] Several of these observers were ideally situated along the flight route between Rabaul and Guadalcanal. With word from the coast watchers of "planes inbound your location," the F4Fs had just enough time to scramble and climb to an advantageous altitude above the enemy formations. The F4Fs had poor climb characteristics at high altitude, and the Cactus pilots needed all 30–40 minutes of warning to reach 28,000 feet.[17] Without advanced warnings from radar and the coast watchers, the Cactus Air Force could have been easily destroyed on the ground like the ill-fated air forces in the Philippines.

Henderson Field provided the Cactus Air Force with a "home field" advantage that muted the superior performance of the Japanese aircraft. The Japanese Zero fighter (Mitsubishi A6M2 Type 0 carrier fighter, Type 21) was much more maneuverable than the F4F Wildcat and, when flown by experienced pilots, the Zeros outmatched the Wildcats in air-to-air combat.[18] Maj John L. Smith, commander of VMF 223, recognized the superiority of the Zeros. He told his pilots to run for Henderson Field or dive into the clouds if Zeros engaged them.[19] Even Marine ace, Capt Joe Foss, stated, "We have a saying up at Guadalcanal, if you're alone and you meet a Zero, run like hell because you're outnumbered."[20] The Zeros were stretched to the limits of their impressive combat range by the four-hour flight from Rabaul. The Japanese fighters simply did not have enough fuel for protracted dogfights. Zeros also could not maneuver at full throttle for fear of ripping off their external tanks and losing their ability to return to Rabaul.[21] Additionally, to reduce fuel consumption, the Zeros were very lightly armored especially when compared to the heavily armored Wildcats. The difference in armament meant that the six 50-caliber machine guns of the F4F usually shredded the Zero, while the Wildcat could survive with multiple bullet holes. Thus, a badly damaged plane from the Cactus Air Force could limp back to Henderson Field, whereas a damaged Zero was more likely to ditch into the ocean than survive the long flight back to Rabaul. In an aerial battle of attrition, the difference between damaged and destroyed aircraft played a key role in the ability to defend Guadalcanal. Rear Adm John S. McCain, commander of Air South Pacific, predicted the future outcome of Guadalcanal in a dispatch sent to Admiral Nimitz: "With substantially the reinforcement requested, Cactus can be a sinkhole for enemy airpower and can be consolidated, expanded, and exploited to enemy's mortal hurt."[22]

The Wildcats avoided tangling with the Zeros when possible because their primary objective was to disrupt the enemy formations before they could bomb the ground troops on Guadalcanal or the transport ships bringing in supplies and reinforcements. Their nemesis was the Japanese medium bomber, the Betty (Mitsubishi Type 1 land-attack plane, model 11), which could fly approximately the same speed as the F4F. The Betty had outstanding range like the Zero, but it sacrificed armored protection to save weight.[23] The 11th Air Fleet, based in Rabaul, launched its Bettys and Zeros in large V formations against Guadalcanal on an almost daily basis during the first months of the campaign. These bombing attacks were so predictable that the men on Guadalcanal called it Tojo time because the attacks almost always struck around noon.[24] To combat these enemy formations, the F4F pilots developed hit-and-run tactics that traded their higher altitude for enough airspeed to overtake the Betty formations. Major Smith developed an overhead-run tactic, which was an almost vertical strafing run that streaked across the bomber formations from right to left.[25] This tactic minimized exposure to the Betty's tail gunners and their fighter escorts. Reinforcements for the Cactus Air Force were almost nonexistent, and the Marine pilots knew they had to keep losses at a minimum while accomplishing their DCA mission. The United States lost 70 F4Fs during air combat from 1 August to 15 November 1942.[26] Total losses in air combat for Japan's 11th Air Fleet during the same period was 72 Zeros and 95 Bettys.[27] Though they were outnumbered and technologically outmatched, American pilots defending Guadalcanal were able to achieve a greater than 2-to-1 kill ratio in air combat. This success can be attributed to timely advanced warning, skillful tactics, and the advantage of fighting near their home base, Henderson Field.[28]

Loss of experienced pilots in aerial battles over Guadalcanal would prove more costly to Japan than their loss of aircraft. Before World War II, Japan had developed a pool of approximately 3,500 highly trained and skilled pilots.[29] The Japanese navy lost hundreds of veteran Sea Eagle pilots in the Battle of Midway, and every Japanese loss in the daily raids over Guadalcanal continued to drain their relatively small pool of experienced pilots.[30] By taking into account the almost 600 miles the Japanese pilots had to cover to return to Rabaul, it can be assumed that most Japanese crews perished when their planes were shot down. Japan's lack of experienced replacements became noticeable to American pilots toward the end of the campaign. As the campaign progressed, American pilots gained experience and confidence in their abilities to fight the Japanese. In contrast to earlier advice to "run from the Zeros," Col Joe "Coach" Bauer spoke to his men before a mission on 23 October and ordered them, "When you see Zeros, dogfight 'em."[31]

In contrast to the loss of Japanese pilots, many American aviators survived after their planes were shot down and returned to the skies to fight the Japanese. Despite a loss of more than 100 planes in combat operations, the Cactus Air Force had only 38 fighter pilots killed in combat.[32] Many Marine fighter aces from the Cactus Air Force were shot down at least once. For instance, Major Smith (credited with 19 victories) crash-landed outside the Marine perimeter after his plane was severely damaged by Zeros on 2 October.[33] Smith claimed, "It was just like a hike," as he avoided Japanese patrols on the six-mile trek back to Henderson Field.[34] Another ace from VMF 223, Capt Marion Carl (credited with 18.5 victories) had his adventure in early September when he bailed out of his burning Wildcat and landed in the waters off Guadalcanal.[35] A native islander saved Captain Carl from the shark-infested waters, and he returned to the American side of the island via boat five days after he was listed as missing and presumed killed in action.[36] Another ace, Maj Robert E. Galer (credited with 14 victories), was shot down twice within three days.[37] Even the top-scoring ace from Guadalcanal, Captain Foss (credited with five victories in one day and 26 victories overall) was shot down and performed a dead-stick landing at Henderson Field.[38] Each of these aces returned to the aerial battle for Guadalcanal in part because of the proximity of Henderson Field, which allowed many pilots to perform dead-stick landings after an unfortunate encounter with the deadly Zero. Thus, in a battle of attrition, the Japanese could not afford the loss of so many experienced pilots while US pilots gained experience and escaped death on multiple occasions.

Tactical Capabilities of Henderson Field—Interdiction

The Cactus Air Force conducted interdiction attacks against Japanese ground forces and naval transports. The primary interdiction mission for the Cactus Air Force was stopping the flow of supplies to the Japanese troops on Guadalcanal. This flow of troops and supplies through the "Slot" (the American name for the channel of water be-

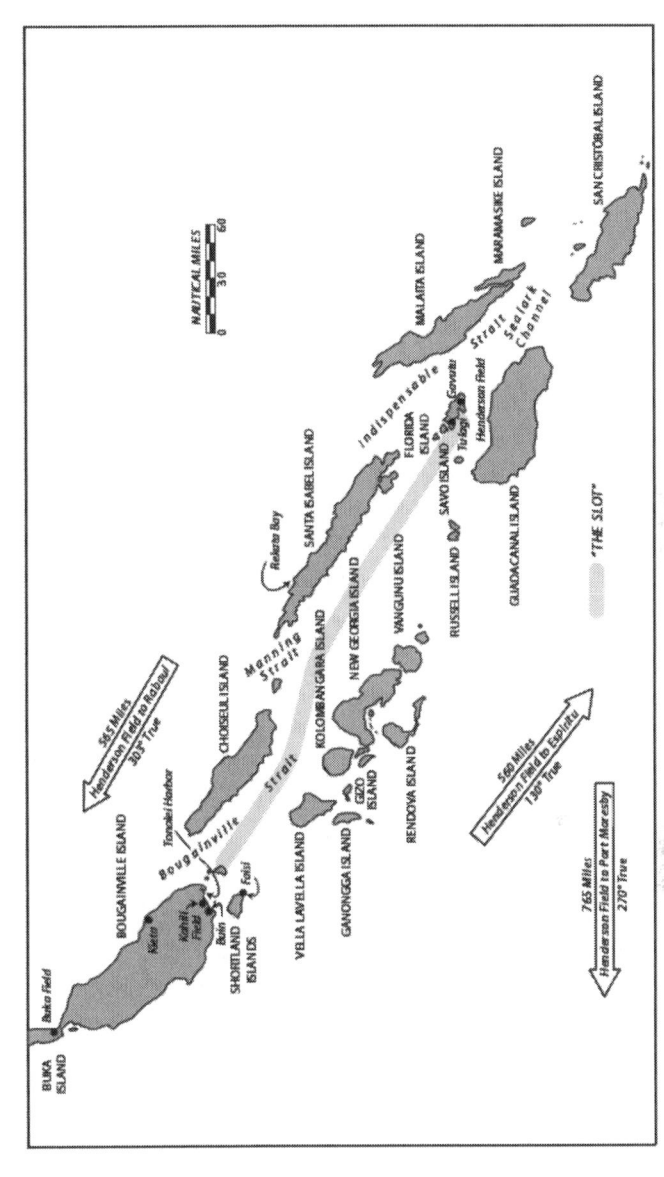

The "Slot" that ran through the Solomon Islands from Bougainville to Guadalcanal. This map also shows the distance from Henderson Field to other major bases such as Rabaul and Port Moresby. (Adapted from *Wings at War Series*, no. 3, *Pacific Counterblow: The 11th Bombardment Group and the 67th Fighter Squadron in the Battle for Guadalcanal*, reprint, Washington, D.C.: Center for Air Force History, 1992.)

tween the Solomon Islands) was called the Tokyo Express because it ran with such regularity. While the Cactus Air Force never halted the Tokyo Express, they did have some success attacking Japanese transport ships, and the Japanese learned that landing supplies during daylight was fruitless.

On 25 August a Japanese convoy was attacked by Marine and Navy SBDs, which sank one transport (*Kinugawa Maru*) and seriously damaged two other ships.[39] Rear Adm Tanaka Raizo, commander of the Japanese convoy, was forced to reverse course with his mangled convoy before he could unload its cargo. In early September Brig Gen Roy Stanley Geiger arrived to command MAW-1 and was determined to put his command on the offensive. On 4 September Geiger ordered his planes to attack any Japanese supply barges they could spot.[40] The next day American planes sank only one of 15 barges, but they killed more than one-half the 700 Japanese infantrymen on the barges during their strafing attacks.[41] This example illustrates the mixed results of the American efforts at interdiction. However, the threat of American airpower forced the Japanese to change their convoy tactics as they virtually abandoned the use of slower transports and barges. The Japanese navy also switched to using their fast destroyers to drop off supplies at night in "rat" operations.[42] These destroyers carried much less cargo but had the advantage of speed, which minimized their time near shore and limited their exposure to air attack.

The Cactus Air Force was truly a joint effort as both Marine and Army pilots flew interdiction missions from Henderson Field. Occasionally, this joint air force was augmented by the arrival of fighter planes from Navy carriers in the South Pacific. These "temporary augmentees" boosted the limited air forces on Guadalcanal and added experienced American combat pilots to the fight. The Navy pilots were useful in finding and attacking naval vessels because they received more training in overwater navigation and ship recognition. Henderson Field was an "unsinkable aircraft carrier" for US Navy pilots in the South Pacific. For example, on 24 August, Lt Turner Caldwell diverted his flight of 11 SBDs into Henderson rather than risk running out of fuel returning to the USS *Enterprise*.[43] These SBDs would join the Marines in their

Kinugawa Maru (Japanese cargo ship). Savo Island is in the distance. (Reprinted from http://www.history.navy.mil/photos/events/wwii-pac/guadlcnl/guadlcnl.htm.)

successful attacks against a Japanese convoy later in August. In early September, Admiral McCain sent all 24 SBDs from Navy Fighter Squadron 5 (VF-5) to augment the Cactus Air Force on Guadalcanal.[44] Upon their arrival, these reinforcements almost doubled the size of the Cactus Air Force. The attack on the Japanese battleship *Hiei* provides another example of carrier aircraft operating from Henderson Field. On 13 November the USS *Enterprise* launched nine Grumman Avenger torpedo bombers to join the attacks on the crippled battleship.[45] The planes landed at Henderson for more fuel and ammunition to reattack the *Hiei*. Upon their landing, the commander of MAW-1, Brig Gen Louis Woods exclaimed, "Boys, I don't know where you came from, but you look like angels dropping out of heaven to us."[46] Eventually, the incessant attacks from Henderson sank the *Hiei*, the first Japanese battleship sunk in the war. The combat skills of the carrier pilots added greatly to the interdiction efforts of the joint air forces at Cactus.

The decisive battle in the Guadalcanal campaign occurred on 14 November, the day after the sinking of the *Hiei*. The Americans expected a major push by the Japanese to reinforce the 17th Army on Guadalcanal. Admiral Tanaka led his convoy of 11 transports and 11 destroyers through the Slot with more than 7,000 troops and tons of supplies.[47] Search planes spotted the convoy early on the 14th, and the first wave of 38 planes launched from Henderson Field around 1100.[48] The American pilots flew wave after wave of attacks against Tanaka's ships until darkness limited flight operations. Fighters from the USS *Enterprise* and B-17s from Espiritu Santo airfield joined the melee of activity over the smoking damaged ships that were desperately maneuvering for protection. Four of the transports avoided damage, and Tanaka decided to beach them at Tassafaronga to get supplies ashore.[49] Planes from Henderson Field returned the following day to attack the beached transports while they were being unloaded. The USS *Meade* joined the fight and shelled the stranded transports with 600 artillery shells for nearly an hour.[50] In the final analysis of the "Air-Naval Battle of Guadalcanal," the Americans achieved a decisive victory because the Japanese lost 10 transports to bring only 2,000 troops, 260 boxes of shells, and 1,500 bags of rice (about a four-day supply) to the destitute 17th Army on Guadalcanal.[51]

Despite successful engagements, the Cactus Air Force and the US Navy never stopped the Tokyo Express. This lack of success was evident by the increase in Japanese troop strength on the island from 2,000 to more than 30,000 over the course of the campaign. The ultimate failure of US efforts to halt Japanese naval operations in the Slot was Japan's successful evacuation of more than 10,000 men from the island in February 1943.[52] The Cactus Air Force remained a constant thorn in the side of Japanese military planners, and US planes succeeded in harassing Japanese supply efforts. The flow of troops and supplies slowed to a trickle as the Japanese were forced to change their tactics to nighttime rat operations. The lack of consistent food supplies and the growing number of troops on the island led to widespread malnutrition among Japanese troops on Guadalcanal. Japanese troops called Guadalcanal "Starvation Island" in reference to the constant lack of rice and other basic supplies. According to one estimate, more than 9,000 Japanese troops died on Guadalcanal from starvation and disease alone.[53] The threat of air interdiction and an occasional victory by the Cactus Air Force made a difference in the difficult logistical struggle that defined the back-and-forth nature of the Guadalcanal campaign.

Tactical Capabilities of Henderson Field—Close Air Support

The Cactus Air Force was used for CAS of the ground troops on Guadalcanal. The Army P-400 was the primary plane used for CAS because it proved woefully inadequate in aerial combat against the superior Zeros. Designed for export, the P-400 lacked the supercharged engine of its P-39 brethren. A lack of suitable oxygen equipment to recharge the P-400's high-pressure oxygen system was the most important factor that limited the plane's dogfighting ability. Without oxygen P-400 pilots could not safely fly above 12,000 feet. At lower altitudes they could not employ the hit-and-run tactics of the Wildcats and were sitting ducks for the Zeros. One pilot wrote that the 67th pilots felt like a "herd of cows being attacked on every flank by agile wolves."[54] After four days of combat, only three P-400s remained in commission from the original group of 14 aircraft.[55] An exasperated General Vandegrift stated the P-400 was "practically worthless for any kind of altitude fighting" and ordered them to conduct CAS and reconnaissance flights only.[56] Admiral McCain informed Admiral Nimitz that the P-400 was "no good at altitude and disheartening to the brave men who fly them."[57] The P-400 was relegated to low-altitude missions, such as strafing Japanese encampments, aerial reconnaissance, and CAS.

As the campaign progressed, the P-400s began conducting CAS missions against the Japanese. These attack pilots became known as the Jagdstaffel, and the Japanese soldiers soon learned to fear the "long-nosed plane."[58] In early September CAS was used during Col Merritt A. Edson's raid on the village of Tasimboko. P-400s and SBDs from Henderson Field dropped bombs on the Japanese positions throughout the morning of the raid, and the P-400s covered the withdrawal of the Marines later that afternoon.[59] During the Battle of Edson's Ridge, the fighting was so close to Henderson Field that three P-400s could circle the runway and provide CAS to halt the Japanese offensive. The unit history of the 67th describes this engagement: "The ground crews could watch the three P-400s at all times, except when they dipped down behind the little hill. Then the murderous chatter of machine guns and cannon could be heard. The plane would pull up, circle the field, then dip down again. Round and round they went, their guns cutting into the massed humanity."[60] Often these CAS missions were successful despite the difficulties of joint operations. An official Marine report highlighted the communication difficulties between the men on the ground and the Army pilots. Messages had to be relayed from the ground force commander to the division command post to Henderson Field and then to the planes overhead the Marines.[61] A couple months after the campaign concluded, General Vandegrift's chief of staff, Col Gerald Thomas, was quoted in *Collier's* magazine as saying that "ground strafing by airplanes killed the most Japs" on Guadalcanal.[62] Thus, despite communication problems, the US Army pilots and their sturdy P-400s proved their value during the campaign through CAS and interdiction.

Force Enablers for Henderson Field—Maintenance

The Cactus Air Force from Henderson Field added the tactical capabilities of DCA, interdiction, and CAS to the Guadalcanal campaign. None of these missions could have occurred without the incredible efforts of maintenance troops at Henderson Field. For instance, in the climatic air-naval battle of Guadalcanal, planes from Henderson Field along with carrier fighters were rapidly refueled and rearmed to launch wave after wave of attacks against the oncoming Japanese convoy. The pace of operations was so demanding that cooks and mess workers were used to help in the efforts to refuel and rearm.[63] This ability to quickly turn fighters for multiple combat missions was a tremendous force multiplier for the relatively small Cactus Air Force.

The story of Cub One from the first days of air operations at Henderson Field provides another example of the tenacity of American maintenance troops. The first planes landed at Henderson several days before their maintenance crews arrived on Guadalcanal. Prior to the arrival of MAG 23, Admiral McCain ordered men from Cub One—a unit designed to establish medium-sized advanced fuel and supply bases—to depart Espiritu Santo and assist the Marines in completing the airfield at Lunga Point.[64] Ens George Polk and 110 men from Cub One arrived at Guadalcanal on 15 August, and they were tasked with servicing the planes at Henderson Field. Because of hasty planning and execution, Henderson Field lacked basic equipment to service fighter aircraft such as fuel pumps and bomb carts. Personnel from Cub One fueled the planes from 55-gallon drums that they tipped by hand into the wing tanks.[65] These ad hoc maintenance troops squatted in the mud under the planes to manually lift the 500- and 1,000-pound bombs into position while the pilots belted the fighter's 50-caliber belts by hand one bullet at a time.[66] Without the yeoman effort by the men of Cub One in the first 12 days of the battle, the Cactus Air Force pilots would not have been able to turn back the Japanese bomber attacks or troop transports bound for Guadalcanal.

In the battle of attrition over Guadalcanal, the ability to repair airplanes and return them to service was absolutely critical to generate the combat capability of the numerically inferior Cactus Air Force. Numerous aircraft performed dead-stick landings at Henderson Field after being damaged during dogfights with the Zeros. Many of these planes were repaired and returned to action, while those that were unsalvageable were used for spare parts. The broken planes were placed in an aircraft boneyard near the field that provided some tactical deception. On one occasion, nine Japanese dive-bombers attacked the planes parked in the aircraft graveyard.[67] In addition to salvaging spare parts, the maintainers also scrounged all the aviation fuel possible from broken planes at Henderson Field. Fuel was always a concern for General Geiger and his staff because the US supply ships had difficulty making it to Guadalcanal unimpeded. At a particularly dire point in October, the maintenance crews siphoned fuel from two B-17s to launch the fighters on one more mission.[68] The unsung work of the maintenance troops kept the planes of the Cactus Air Force flying in spite of the extremely rugged living conditions on the island.

Force Enablers for Henderson Field—Runway Construction and Repair

The ability to construct and then repair the airfield enabled the Cactus Air Force to fly in terrible conditions. For instance, the Marine engineering battalion performed magnificently to complete a 180-foot gap in the airfield in less than two weeks. The construction crews used captured Japanese equipment such as road rollers and handcarts to move 6,700 cubic feet of dirt and gravel to complete the airfield.[69] The engineers also improved the approaches to the field by blasting away some dense jungle foliage. The Marines were relieved of their runway maintenance duties by the arrival of almost 400 Seabees from the 6th Naval Construction Battalion on 1 September.[70] The Seabees quickly improved the landing surface of Henderson Field by placing perforated metal planks called Marston Mat over an improved base of gravel, coral, and clay. By 9 September the Seabees also completed an auxiliary field, called Fighter One or the cow pasture, of mowed Kunai grass that was used by lightweight fighters for the rest of the campaign.[71] The ability to rapidly construct the expeditionary airfields on Guadalcanal enabled the United States to begin air operations from Henderson Field less than two weeks after the amphibious assault landed at Red Beach.

Henderson Field was a prime target for the Japanese throughout the struggle for control of Guadalcanal. Henderson Field was a static target that represented the source of much of the Japanese military's frustration with taking Guadalcanal back from the Americans. The ability of the Seabees to rapidly repair damage to Henderson Field's runways was absolutely vital to maintaining a steady pace of combat sorties against the Japanese. According to Joseph Blundon, commander of the Seabee battalion, 100 Seabees could repair a crater from a 500-pound bomb and replace the Marston Mat in 40 minutes.[72] For example, the bombardment of Henderson Field highlights the important contributions made by the Seabees. In preparation for a major offensive, the Japanese conducted a major attack on Henderson Field during the night of 13–14 October. That night, in addition to aerial bombing and artillery shelling, two Japanese battleships rained 918, 14-inch shells on the Marine base and Henderson Field.[73] This shelling, known as the bombardment, was described in one historical account as follows: "Heavy shells crashed into the gasoline storage and ammunition dump, while all over the field the aircraft went up in clouds of smoke and flame. In hundreds of foxholes and improvised bomb shelters, men clung to the ground, cursing, praying, and in some cases, going out of their minds."[74] The morning after the bombardment, Henderson Field was unusable and only seven of 39 SBDs were flyable.[75] Fortunately, the Cactus Air Force had Fighter One—which was not damaged by the shelling—and 24 Wildcats remained available along with six Army Air Force P-400s and P-39s.[76] After the bombardment, the Seabees had their work cut out for them as Commander Blundon described afterward: "During one hour on the 14th, we filled 13 bomb craters while our planes circled overhead waiting to land. We got no food during that period because our cooks were all busy passing up the steel plank. There were not enough shovels to go around, so some of our men used their helmets to scoop up earth and carry it to the bomb craters."[77] The almost daily shelling from artillery, bombers, and ships did not deter the Seabees's extraordinary efforts to keep Henderson Field operational for the Cactus Air Force.

Force Enablers for Henderson Field—Airfield Security

In addition to completing the construction of Henderson Field, General Vandegrift knew his primary mission was the security of the airfield.[78] By mid-September, the Marines devised an ingenious scheme of defense for the entire perimeter of Henderson Field. Rather than building a textbook "defense in depth," the Marines used a thin cordon of troops to deny Japanese infiltration. The tactics relied on the Marines' ability to mass superior firepower against the Japanese with their rifles, mortars, and artillery.[79] In his final report on the Guadalcanal operation, General Vandegrift stated, "There was never any occasion to regret the decision to employ the perimeter type of defense, and, on one occasion at least it saved us from a disastrous surprise."[80] These novel tactics would be tested by the Japanese infantry, but the Marines demonstrated a "bend but don't break" attitude and fiercely defended the air base. By the end of September—when Admiral Nimitz visited the island—General Vandegrift impressed upon him that holding Henderson Field remained his main mission.[81]

During the six-month campaign, the Marines engaged the Japanese in several pitched battles to defend Henderson Field. During the Battle of Edson's Ridge (also known as Battle of Bloody Ridge), the Marines repelled three separate waves of Japanese infantry to hold a ridge just one mile south of the airfield. The Marines fell back toward the airfield and, at one point, the Japanese were within 1,000 yards of Henderson Field. In that battle, the Japanese suffered 1,138 casualties compared to 143 for the Marines.[82] Another pitched ground battle for control of Henderson Field occurred in late October. During the Battle for Henderson Field, the Japanese sought to exploit the success of the earlier bombardment. Again, the Japanese sought to overwhelm the Marines by throwing wave after wave of shrieking infantry into the lines. At the main point of attack, the Japanese outnumbered the Marines by nine to one.[83] Once again, the Marines used superior firepower from their artillery and mortars to halt the Japanese offensive, causing another 2,200 Japanese casualties. These battles are just two examples of the tenacious and brutal fighting that occurred in the defense of Henderson Field.

Force Enablers for Henderson Field—Logistics

The logistics planning for Operation Watchtower was so poor that some people used the tongue-in-cheek term *Operation Shoestring* when referring to Guadalcanal. The hasty planning and extreme distances in the Pacific made the supply of fresh troops, food, fuel, and ammunition difficult at best. Naval shipping carried almost all of the supplies and troops to Guadalcanal. However, the Japanese air force and navy made life difficult for Admiral Kelly and his transports. Air transport was used to bring in supplies at critical times. For instance, after the bombardment destroyed all the aviation fuel at Henderson Field, General Vandegrift's dispatch to Admiral Ghormley stated, "Absolutely essential aviation gas be flown here continuously."[84] The next day, C-47 transport planes from Espiritu Santo brought 12 55-gallon drums of fuel each (one drum was enough for a one-hour flight) to sustain marginal air operations.[85]

In addition to bringing in routine supplies such as candy, cigarettes, and spare parts, cargo planes flying into Henderson Field were also regularly used to evacuate medical patients.[86] General Vandegrift also summed up his appreciation for air transport: "I would like to pay tribute to those men who flew the DC-3s in day after day with no protection whatsoever, and who saved us innumerable worries as to critical supplies. They came in with supplies and went out with the wounded."[87] In a campaign held together by a shoestring, the ability to bring in supplies by air provided just enough logistics support at key times to sustain the fighting forces until the next transport ship arrived.

Relevance of Guadalcanal—Then

The American victory at Guadalcanal was a turning point in the war against Japan on many levels. At the tactical level, the Japanese failed to gather sufficient force in the first few weeks of the campaign to dislodge the Americans from Guadalcanal. In August the Japanese underestimated the size of the American occupation force and sent only piecemeal reinforcements to Guadalcanal because their focus was capturing Port Moresby. The Japanese military leaders failed to realize at the outset that the expeditionary airfield was a COG. They missed an opportunity to capitalize on the hasty planning of the Americans and strike before the airfield was operational. A Marine Corps report following the war illustrates this point: "During this critical period [from 9 August to 20 August] the enemy enjoyed unchallenged supremacy at sea and in the air and subjected our positions to constant attack from both elements. Had the enemy perceived or been able to take full advantage of this favorable opportunity by moving in force from Rabaul and Truk, it would have become difficult, if not impossible, to maintain our positions."[88] By late August, the Japanese high command made the recapture of Guadalcanal a top priority.[89] After their defeat during the Battle of Edson's Ridge, the Japanese Supreme War Council made Guadalcanal their top priority, and they assigned more troops to the campaign.[90] After weeks of battle, the Japanese military leaders finally recognized that destroying Henderson Field and thereby eliminating the threat of American airpower was a critical step in achieving their objectives, but it was too late.

The United States and Japan stood toe-to-toe for months and traded blows during the many battles of the Guadalcanal campaign. However, as the campaign continued, the United States gained tactical experience, and the grueling test of combat honed the fighting edge of the US forces. The victories in the air and on the ground at Guadalcanal proved to the Americans that the Japanese were fierce in combat, but they could be defeated. These victories might appear minor, but they led to a growth in confidence that was reflected by the change in tactics of running from Zeros in August to fighting them by late October. Ultimately, the defeat at Guadalcanal cost the Japanese much more than lost territory, destroyed planes, and damaged ships. By most accounts, the biggest cost of the grinding battle of attrition was that Japan lost too many experienced pilots, sailors, and troops whose skills they simply could not replace. An ironic footnote to the Guadalcanal campaign is that Adm Isoroku Yamamoto, the mastermind of the attack on Pearl Harbor, was killed on 18 April 1943 when his plane was shot down by a flight of Army P-38s launched from Henderson Field.[91]

Operationally, the American victory at Guadalcanal marked the beginning of the drive to roll back the Japanese advance. During the Guadalcanal campaign, the Americans gained experience in jungle combat, operating from an expeditionary base and other important lessons that would pay dividends later in the war. For example, the use of expeditionary airfields became the template for future island-hopping operations in the South Pacific. In a February 1943 interview, General Vandegrift stated, "We must conclude that the rest of this campaign in the South Pacific—practically to its conclusion—will be the seizure of islands, either to take away from the enemy, airdromes which they hold, or to seize other islands to make airdromes of our own."[92] Following this template, Gen George Kenney, the commander of allied air forces in the Southwest Pacific, established expeditionary air bases throughout the theater to place his fighters and bombers closer to the Japanese positions.[93] The Americans also knew that remote air bases were a COG for the enemy and attacked them whenever possible. For instance, in December 1942, the Japanese built an airfield at Munda on the island of New Georgia (170 miles from Guadalcanal). The Japanese attempted to camouflage their construction work through various methods such as stringing up palm trees to cover the runway.[94] In spite of these concealment efforts, planes from Henderson Field bombed the field daily and destroyed many Zeros on the ground. By the end of December, the Japanese abandoned the airfield at Munda because they could not afford the high losses.[95] Thus, using expeditionary airfields and denying the enemy access to expeditionary airfields was a central part of the American operational strategy in the Southwest Pacific during World War II.

At the strategic level, the American victory over Japan shook the confidence of Japanese leadership at the highest levels. The significance of a small island in the South Pacific grew as more effort and energy were put into the campaign by both sides. The Japanese commitment of more than 31,000 troops to recapture Guadalcanal only raised the ultimate cost of losing the campaign. By October the American leadership finally grasped the importance of succeeding in the campaign when Pres. Franklin D. Roosevelt directed the JCS "to make sure that every possible weapon gets into that area to hold Guadalcanal."[96] While both countries committed significant resources to the campaign, the overall Japanese losses were remarkably higher. The Japanese Imperial Army alone lost more than 20,000 men, while the US casualties on the island were 1,207 Marines and 562 Army soldiers.[97] Maj

Gen Kiyotak Kawaguchi summed up the Japanese mood: "Guadalcanal is not the name of an island. It is the name of the graveyard of the Japanese army."[98] The Japanese military lost its aura of invincibility as it suffered the first taste of defeat after a prolonged campaign. Japan never regained the initiative after the defeat at Guadalcanal and fought on the strategic defensive for the remainder of World War II.

Relevance of Guadalcanal—Now

The successful defense of Henderson Field and the American victory in the Guadalcanal campaign have relevant lessons for current military planners. The war against terrorism and events of the past few years emphasize the importance of global operations. By one official estimate, the US Air Force has established 36 operational air bases since 11 September 2001.[99] In many countries the expeditionary airfield is the critical link that allows US forces access to a theater of operations. For instance, in Operation Iraqi Freedom the United States captured and used airfields throughout Iraq to expedite the movement of forces and open multiple fronts in that campaign. Even Baghdad International Airport was used as an expeditionary airfield for US forces. Gen John J. Jumper, the Air Force chief of staff, believes the "natural state" for the US Air Force is deployed operations.[100] The expeditionary airfield provides access for US forces, and it serves as a platform for the forward projection of airpower into a theater. The expeditionary airfield is a source of strength, or COG, for the US military.

The importance of expeditionary airfields to modern military operations can be compared to the role Henderson Field played in the Guadalcanal campaign. For instance, Bagram Air Base (AB) is one of two major US expeditionary airfields in the landlocked country of Afghanistan. In the early months of Operation Enduring Freedom, Bagram AB was the only way to provide supplies and troop reinforcements to US forces in Northern Afghanistan. As at Henderson Field, injured troops are medically evacuated by air from Bagram. All of the combat force enablers, such as civil engineering and maintenance, are absolutely vital to Bagram's air operations. US Air Force civil engineers from RED HORSE (Rapid Engineer Deployable Heavy Operations Repair Squadron Engineers) had to repair the Bagram runway, which suffered extensive damage from bombs, small munitions, and an overall lack of care and maintenance. The RED HORSE team used approximately 2,500 cubic yards of concrete to fix the more than 500 individual slabs that make up the runway.[101] Currently, attack aircraft (e.g., the A-10 and Apache helicopter) use the repaired runway to provide CAS for US and coalition ground forces fighting against Taliban and al-Qaeda forces in Afghanistan. Obviously, Bagram AB and Henderson Field have differences such as improvements in technology and the absence of a substantial threat to Bagram. Yet these two airfields share many similarities; these common threads demonstrate the continued importance of expeditionary airfields to the operational art of war.

The US Air Force has recognized the importance of expeditionary airfields after the widespread use of them during recent military operations in Iraq and Afghanistan. The Air Force recently instituted a new flag-level training exercise, Eagle Flag, to improve expeditionary combat-support skills. According to Maj Gen Christopher Kelly, the commander of the Air Mobility Warfare Center, Eagle Flag will test expeditionary combat-support leadership's ability to establish an air base in an austere location.[102] Like Red Flag, the goal of Eagle Flag exercises is to develop these critical skills in peacetime so that if they are needed in a future combat situation, then the service members are not facing this challenge for the first time. Henderson Field events illustrated how the many different elements of combat support enabled the use of airpower from an austere airfield. The strength of American airpower simply cannot be unleashed unless planes are fixed, fueled, and armed. The airfield perimeter must be secured, and the runway must be serviceable. Thus, one of the most important lessons from the experiences at Henderson Field was that, in war, sometimes a bulldozer is more important than a single fighter plane.

Conclusion

Henderson Field provides a historical example of the expeditionary airfield as a COG for joint military operations. Henderson Field was the hub for the Cactus Air Force, which included planes and pilots from every branch of service. Operating under austere conditions that defined the South Pacific islands, the Cactus Air Force provided several critical capabilities, including DCA, to defeat daily bombing attacks from the Japanese. The Cactus Air Force also conducted interdiction attacks against Japanese naval supply convoys and encampments on the island. CAS was another combat capability provided by the Cactus Air Force. In this case, the air-to-air weakness of the P-400 was turned into an advantage because these planes were very effective at low-altitude attacks.

Henderson Field's historical record also demonstrates that key force enablers provide critical capabilities for the use of airpower from austere airfields. Specifically, aircraft maintenance and runway repair are two support functions that were absolutely vital to air operations in the grueling battle of attrition that defined the Guadalcanal campaign. Airfield security was another key force enabler. The US Marine Corps, and later the US Army, defended the airfield against multiple Japanese offensives, which were characterized by waves of banzai attackers. Henderson Field also allowed air transport to perform a key support role when fuel supplies were scarce and when wounded soldiers needed medical evacuation. In a letter to the First Marine Division, General Vandegrift summarized the contributions of the Cactus Air Force: "Operating under difficulties from an unfinished advanced air base with limited facilities for upkeep and repair of these units [VMSB-232, VMF-223, VF-5, and the 67th FS] have without regard for the cost sought out the enemy at every opportunity and have engaged him with such aggressiveness and skill as to contribute conspicuously to the success of the Allied cause in the Solomon Island area."[103]

The American victory at Guadalcanal and the use of expeditionary air bases had immediate ramifications for the war in the Pacific. The use of island air bases as unsinkable carriers in the Pacific served as the template for US military operations in the Southwest Pacific during the remainder of World War II. The victory at Guadalcanal boosted the American soldiers' confidence, and the US military gained valuable experience in jungle warfare. In contrast, the loss cost Japan thousands of experienced soldiers and skilled pilots. Subsequent to Guadalcanal, Japan did not regain the strategic offensive for the rest of the war.

The experience at Henderson Field during the Guadalcanal campaign has relevance to current US military planners. In the global war against terrorism, expeditionary operations are the norm as demonstrated by Operations Enduring Freedom and Iraqi Freedom. In this context, the expeditionary air base will remain a COG for joint military operations. These air bases, placed in austere locations, bring the combat capabilities of American airpower to the theater of operations. Combat support for expeditionary air bases is also absolutely essential as demonstrated by recent Eagle Flag exercises. Key enablers such as maintenance and civil engineering allow airpower to operate seamlessly from these less-than-ideal locations.

The historical example of Henderson Field contains relevant lessons for future expeditionary military operations in the global war against terrorism. The petition signed by thousands of veterans from World War II demonstrated that they have not forgotten the significance of an austere airfield located on a small island in the South Pacific. In August 2003, the prime minister of the Solomon Islands responded to their petition by promising that the name of the airport on Guadalcanal would remain Honiara International Airport–Henderson Field.[104]

Notes

Most of the notes appear in shortened form. For full details, see the appropriate entries in the bibliography.

1. Christie, "Solomons Airport Still a Battlefield 60 Years On."
2. Joint Publication 3-0, *Doctrine for Joint Operations*, III-22.
3. Frank, *Guadalcanal*, 34–35.
4. Ibid., 36.
5. Schom, *The Eagle and the Rising Sun*, 325.
6. This landing was the first amphibious assault by the US Marine Corps since 1898 in the Spanish–American War.
7. Frank, *Guadalcanal*, 599.
8. Ibid., 81.

9. Ibid., 59.
10. Lundstrom, *The First Team and the Guadalcanal Campaign*, 81 and 84–85. Admiral Fletcher's decision to withdraw his carrier forces was one of the reasons that he was court-martialed for cowardice by the Navy in 1943. Thus, Fletcher has been widely condemned by most writers on this topic. However, Lundstrom makes a few points in defense of Fletcher's decision.
11. Schom, *The Eagle and the Rising Sun*, 345–46. In the 33-minute attack, the Japanese surface force, led by Vice Adm Gunichi Mikawa, sank four heavy cruisers and damaged three other US ships. The Battle of Savo Island has been labeled the "worst naval defeat in US history."
12. Schom, *The Eagle and the Rising Sun*, 347. According to Frank, General Vandegrift had 10,819 men on Guadalcanal and 6,075 men on Tulagi. Admiral Turner's convoy departed with almost 1,800 Marines still aboard the transports. See also Frank, *Guadalcanal*, 125.
13. Frank, *Guadalcanal*, 127.
14. Ibid.
15. Vandegrift and Asprey, *Once a Marine*, 139.
16. Rohfleisch, *Guadalcanal and the Origins of the Thirteenth Air Force*, 102–4.
17. Lundstrom, *The First Team*, 201.
18. Ibid., 43–44.
19. Miller, *The Cactus Air Force*, 72.
20. Mersky, *Time of the Aces*, 19.
21. Ibid., 73.
22. Ibid., 65.
23. Lundstrom, *The First Team*, 43.
24. Dillon, *History of the 67th Fighter Squadron*, 27.
25. Miller, *The Cactus Air Force*, 72.
26. Frank, *Guadalcanal*, 646.
27. Ibid., 645.
28. This record of success is even more impressive when living conditions for the pilots on Guadalcanal are taken into consideration. The pilots suffered through same conditions as the Marines who were defending the field, such as nightly shelling or bombing from the ever-present "Washing Machine Charlie" bomber, widespread disease such as malaria, and an overall lack of food. These conditions prevented sleep at night, and pilot fatigue was common. It is said that men on Guadalcanal flew under conditions when most of them would have been grounded by the flight surgeon. See Rohfleisch, *Guadalcanal and the Origins of the Thirteenth Air Force*, 187–88.
29. Frank, *Guadalcanal*, 66.
30. By most estimates, the United States entered the war with twice as many naval aviators as Japan. During the initial stages of the war, the United States produced a new pilot in months versus Japan's pilot-training program, which took years to produce a single pilot.
31. Miller, *The Cactus Air Force*, 139.
32. Ibid., 209.
33. Ibid., 103.
34. Ibid.
35. Mersky, *Time of the Aces*, 6.
36. Miller, *The Cactus Air Force*, 92. When General Geiger learned of Captain Carl's return, he informed him that Major Smith—his squadron commander and rival for kills—had shot down 16 planes to Carl's 12.

When Geiger asked him what he was going to do about that, Carl replied, "General, ground him for five days!"

37. Mersky, *Time of the Aces*, 6.
38. Miller, *The Cactus Air Force*, 117.
39. Frank, *Guadalcanal*, 190–92.
40. Miller, *The Cactus Air Force*, 76.
41. Ibid.
42. Frank, *Guadalcanal*, 199. Each destroyer could only carry about 150 troops and 30–40 tons of supplies.
43. Lundstrom, *The First Team*, 155.
44. Ibid., 181.
45. Ibid., 478.
46. Ibid., 481.
47. Ibid., 498.
48. Ibid., 499.
49. Frank, *Guadalcanal*, 487.
50. Rohfleisch, *Guadalcanal and the Origins of the Thirteenth Air Force*, 62.
51. Ibid., 490–91.
52. Schom, *The Eagle and the Rising Sun*, 454.
53. Hammel, *Guadalcanal–Starvation Island*, 450.
54. Dillon, *History of the 67th Fighter Squadron*, 11.
55. Craven and Cate, *The Army Air Forces in World War II*, 41.
56. Vandegrift and Asprey, *Once a Marine*, 145.
57. Miller, *The Cactus Air Force*, 65–66.
58. *Wings at War Series*, 25–28.
59. Miller, *The Cactus Air Force*, 79–80.
60. Dillon, *History of the 67th Fighter Squadron*, 23.
61. *An Evaluation of Air Operations Affecting the US Marine Corps in World War II*, III-18.
62. Dillon, *History of the 67th Fighter Squadron*, 20.
63. Lundstrom, *The First Team*, 511.
64. Mersky, *Time of the Aces*, 3.
65. Ibid.
66. Rohfleisch, *Guadalcanal and the Origins of the Thirteenth Air Force*, 38.
67. Frank, *Guadalcanal*, 360.
68. Rohfleisch, *Guadalcanal and the Origins of the Thirteenth Air Force*, 37.
69. Frank, *Guadalcanal*, 127.
70. Morison, *The Struggle for Guadalcanal*, 76.
71. Miller, *The Cactus Air Force*, 82. The Seabees would eventually complete two auxiliary fields around Henderson Field. For simplicity, all of the US airfields at Lunga Point are included when referring to Henderson Field in this study, unless specifically delineated.
72. Huie, *Can Do!* 41–42. The Seabees figured out how much sand and gravel was required to fill the average bomb or shell crater. They would load these premeasured amounts onto trucks parked strategically around the airfield.
73. Ibid., 118.
74. Rohfleisch, *Guadalcanal and the Origins of the Thirteenth Air Force*, 34.
75. Frank, *Guadalcanal*, 319.
76. Ibid.
77. Huie, *Can Do!* 42.

78. Frank, *Guadalcanal*, 125.
79. Ibid., 261–63.
80. Commanding General, First Marine Division, Fleet Marine Force, *Final Report on the Guadalcanal Operation*, 3.
81. Vandegrift and Asprey, *Once a Marine*, 171.
82. Schom, *The Eagle and the Rising Sun*, 367.
83. Frank, *Guadalcanal*, 366.
84. Miller, *The Cactus Air Force*, 123.
85. Rohfleisch, *Guadalcanal and the Origins of the Thirteenth Air Force*, 38.
86. Ibid., 110.
87. Maj Gen Alexander Archer Vandegrift, US Marine Corps, interview by the author, 3 February 1943, 9.
88. *An Evaluation of Air Operations Affecting the US Marine Corps in World War II*, III-10.
89. Schom, *The Eagle and the Rising Sun*, 362.
90. Ibid., 367.
91. Miller, *The Cactus Air Force*, 206–7.
92. Vandegrift, interview, 1.
93. Ibid., 436.
94. Frank, *Guadalcanal*, 525.
95. Ibid., 526.
96. Ibid., 392.
97. Ibid., 613.
98. Twining, *No Bended Knee*, ix.
99. Fazzini, "Inaugural Eagle Flag Concludes."
100. Jumper, "Chief's Sight Picture."
101. D'Andrea, "RED HORSE Improves Runways."
102. Fazzini, "Air Force Will Test Eagle Flag."
103. Vandegrift and Asprey, *Once a Marine*, 145–46.
104. Kemakeza, letter, 20 August 2003.

Bibliography

Christie, Michael. "Solomons Airport Still a Battlefield 60 Years On," 28 July 2003. http://www.pacificwrecks.com/ new/henderson/reuters.html (accessed 27 March 2004).

Commanding General, First Marine Division, Fleet Marine Force. *Final Report on the Guadalcanal Operation,* 19 September–9 December 1942, in the USAF collection, Air Force Historical Research Agency (AFHRA), Maxwell AFB, Ala., 180.1-1, pt. 5.

Craven, Wesley Frank, and James Lea Cate, eds. *The Army Air Forces in World War II.* Vol. 4, *The Pacific: Guadalcanal to Saipan, August 1942 to July 1944.* 1949. New imprint, Washington, D.C.: Office of Air Force History, 1983.

D'Andrea, Christa. "RED HORSE Improves Runways, Housing in Afghanistan," 8 August 2002. http://www/af.mil/news/story_print.asp?storyID=8080270 (accessed 12 March 2004).

Dillon, Barclay, Jr. *History of the 67th Fighter Squadron,* pts., 2–3. SQ-FI-67-H1, 16 January 1941–31 December 1943, in the USAF Collection, AFHRA.

Evaluation of Air Operations Affecting the US Marine Corps in World War II, An. Quantico, Va.: Marine Corps Schools, 1945.

Fazzini, Paul. "Air Force Will Test Eagle Flag," 3 October 2003.

———. "Inaugural Eagle Flag Concludes," 22 October 2003. http://www.af.mil/stories/story.asp?storyID=123005858 (12 March 2004).

Frank, Richard B. *Guadalcanal: The Definitive Account of the Landmark Battle.* New York: Penguin Books, 1990.

Hammel, Eric. *Guadalcanal–Starvation Island.* Pacifica, Calif.: Pacifica Press, 1987. http://www.af.mil/stories/story.asp?storyID=123005728 (accessed 12 March 2004).

Huie, William Bradford. *Can Do! The Story of the Seabees.* New York: E. P. Dutton and Co., 1944.

Joint Publication 3-0. *Doctrine for Joint Operations,* 10 September 2001.

Jumper, John J. "Chief's Sight Picture: The Culture of Our Air and Space Expeditionary Force and the Value of Air Force Doctrine." http://www.af.mil/media/viewpoints/AEFfinal.pdf (accessed 1 April 2004).

Kemakeza, Prime Minister, Allan, Solomon Islands. To Petition Signers and Veterans. Letter, 20 August 2003. http://pacificwrecks.com/news/henderson/pm-letter.html (accessed 27 March 2004).

Lundstrom, John B. *The First Team and the Guadalcanal Campaign: Naval Fighter Combat from August to November 1942.* Annapolis: Naval Institute Press, 1994.

Mersky, Peter B. *Time of the Aces: Marine Pilots in the Solomons.* Washington, D.C.: Marine Corps Historical Center, 1993.

Miller, Thomas G., Jr. *The Cactus Air Force.* New York: Harper and Row, 1969.

Morison, Samuel Eliot. *History of United States Naval Operations in World War II.* Vol. 5, *The Struggle for Guadalcanal August 1942–February 1943.* 1948. Reprint, Boston: Little, Brown and Co., 1989.

Rohfleisch, Kramer J. *Guadalcanal and the Origins of the Thirteenth Air Force* (U), 8 June 1959. Army Air Forces Historical Studies, no. 35, 1945. 101-35 in the USAF Collection, AFHRA.

Schom, Alan. *The Eagle and the Rising Sun: The Japanese–American War, 1941–1943, Pearl Harbor through Guadalcanal.* New York: W. W. Norton and Co., 2004.

Twining, Merrill B. *No Bended Knee: The Battle for Guadalcanal, The Memoir of Gen. Merrill B. Twining, USMC (Ret.).* Edited by Neil Carey. Novato, Calif.: Presidio Press, 1996.

Vandegrift, A. A., and Robert B. Asprey. *Once a Marine: The Memoirs of General A. A. Vandegrift.* New York: W. W. Norton and Co., 1964.

Wings at War Series, No. 3. Pacific Counterblow: The 11th Bombardment Group and the 67th Fighter Squadron in the Battle for Guadalcanal. New Imprint. Washington, D.C.: Center for Air Force History, 1992.

Vandegrift, Alexander Archer. Interview, 3 February 1943. Transcript. USAF Collection. AFHRA document 142.052.

Appendix A

US Marine Corps Aces from Guadalcanal

Joe Foss (26 confirmed kills).
http://www.acesandautographs.com/USMCacephotos.htm

Robert Galer (14 confirmed kills).
http://www.au.af.mil/au/goe/indexpages/eagleindexpage.htm

Marion Carl (18.5 confirmed kills).
http://www.daveswarbirds.com/cactus/cactus.htm

http://www.acesandautographs.com/USMCacephotos.htm

Maj John Smith (19 confirmed kills).
http://www.daveswarbirds.com/cactus/cactus.htm

Left to right: Maj John L. Smith, Maj Robert E. Galer, and Capt Marion E. Carl, after just having been decorated with the Navy Cross by Admiral Nimitz on 1 October 1942. They are wearing blue baseball caps that were part of the uniform of Cactus pilots (http://www.daveswarbirds.com/cactus/cactus.htm).

Appendix B

The Planes of the Cactus Air Force

Guadalcanal Campaign, 1942–1943. Marine Corps Grumman F4F Wildcat fighter at Henderson Field, 2 February 1943. Markings under the cockpit indicate that this plane has been credited with shooting down 19 Japanese aircraft, while being flown by several different pilots (http://www.history.navy.mil/photos/events/wwii-pac/guadlcnl/guadlcnl.htm).

Giving Her the Once-Over. 2d Lt Barclay Dillon of the 67th Fighter Squadron tends to his P-400 (http://www.daveswarbirds.com/cactus/cactus.htm).

Another Mission Begins. A group of Dauntlesses (SBDs) line up for takeoff prior to another mission. Note that the runway is made of interlocking pieces of PSP (pierced steel planking), also called Marston matting. This gave the runways a solid surface when the ground turned to mud (http://www.daveswarbirds.com/cactus/cactus.htm).

Two Down, More to Go. An SBD is silhouetted against a sky filling with smoke from two Japanese ships knocked out in air attacks against these and other ships of the Tokyo Express, which were attempting to bring Japanese troop reinforcements to the island (http://www.daveswarbirds.com/cactus/cactus.htm).

Patrolling Cactus Airspace. A pair of Wildcats cruise over Guadalcanal. It was not uncommon for pilots in World War II to fly with the canopy open while not engaged in combat (http://www.daveswarbirds.com/cactus/cactus.htm).

Appendix C

Combat Support on Guadalcanal

Repairing the Marston Matting. Day and night, Japanese planes attacked Henderson Field. Here US Navy, Marine, and Army men band together to repair the bomb-wrecked steel-matted runway (http://www.daveswarbirds.com/cactus/cactus.htm).

Right, Col Joe Bauer visually describes his dogfight to his dedicated ground crew. He was the commander of Marine Fighter Squadron 212 at Guadalcanal. Known as "Indian Joe" and as the "Coach," he was immensely respected for his combat flying and leadership abilities. Just before his tour of Guadalcanal was to end, he went on his last mission, was shot down, and is believed to have succumbed to the dangers of the waters off of the Russell Islands (near Guadalcanal). He was posthumously awarded the Congressional Medal of Honor.

Appendix D

Expeditionary Air Operations—Then

Aircobra Scramble. A P-400 rolls past a B-17 as it prepares to take to the air. Members of the 6th Seabees pause momentarily in their work to watch the takeoff (http://www.daveswarbirds.com/cactus/cactus.htm).

Appendix E

Expeditionary Air Operations—Now

C-17 Globemaster III taking off from Bagram Air Base in Afghanistan while Air Force Civil Engineers repair the end of the runway (http://www.boeing.com/news/frontiers/archive/2002/may/qt_snapshots.html).

Printed in Great Britain
by Amazon